I. INTRODUCTION

The past decade has witnessed remarkable developments in the quantitative analysis of horizontal mergers. Several factors account for these changes. The quantity and quality of data available to estimate the degree of substitutability among competing products has increased dramatically. This increase has been accompanied by a substantial decrease in the price of computing power required to analyze the data. A third factor is an increased focus on the possibility of competitive harm from "unilateral" market conduct, particularly in mergers involving differentiated products. However, understanding how consumers substitute among competing products also can contribute substantially to the analysis of possible competitive harm from "coordinated" market behavior.

How consumers substitute across products as relative prices change is clearly relevant to understanding the potential price effects of mergers.[1] This information, contained in the own- and cross-price elasticities of demand at retail,[2] is most frequently used as means for predicting the "unilateral" incentives to increase prices post-merger. In the context of differentiated consumer goods, the term "unilateral effects" refers to the fact that a merger of competitors creates an incentive to increase price (*ceteris paribus*) to the extent that there are significant substitution possibilities that exist between the (now) jointly-owned products. In this setting, the existence of credible information about demand elasticities is clearly important. Having a good estimate of how substitutable these products are can help the analyst predict with much greater accuracy whether these unilateral incentives to raise price are substantial or minuscule.[3]

---

[1] Of course the own- and cross-price elasticities of the demand faced by manufacturers ("wholesale demand") is more directly relevant to Guidelines market definition and competitive effects analyses. The properties of demand of consumers (*i.e.*, the demand at retail) is relevant because they have implications for the demand at the manufacturer level.

[2] The elasticity of some variable x with respect to another variable y is the percentage change in x that arises from a 1% increase in y. For example, the own-price elasticity of the demand for widgets is the percentage change in the quantity of widgets given a 1% increase in their price.

[3] It has become conventional to analyze these unilateral pricing incentives using static oligopoly models in which firms compete on the basis of price. The static oligopoly game that models firms' pricing decisions is sometimes referred to as the "Bertrand" pricing game after Joseph Bertrand (1883), who was the first economist to study it. This is the framework used most often to examine unilateral effects in merger analysis. Whether these static models provide an appropriate benchmark for predicting the consequences of a horizontal merger is somewhat controversial (see, e.g., Fisher (1989) and Shapiro (1989)); we do not address this controversy here. We note, however, the recent appearance of studies that attempt to test the validity of static oligopoly models (e.g., Nevo (2001); Pinske and Slade (2001); Hausman and Leonard (2000); Genesove and Mullin (1998); Wolfram (1999)). Most of these studies suggest that the static oligopoly models yield reasonably accurate predictions of pricing behavior.

Until quite recently, economists had to rely on relatively simple quantitative analyses (surveys, analysis of shift in share, *etc.*) and qualitative information (for example, an internal company document stating that products X, Y, and Z all compete with each other) – that did not permit quantification of the degree of substitutability among the merging firms' products. While these sources of information are useful and continue to play an important role in merger analysis, a well-executed econometric analysis of demand may enable an economist to infer not only that a set of goods are substitutes, but also to infer *what volume of sales* will switch from product X to product Y given (say) a specific price increase for product X.

The value of information on demand elasticities is not limited to situations where attention is focused primarily on unilateral pricing incentives. Evidence bearing on the degree of substitutability among potentially competing products is also important in determining the incentive and ability to engage in coordinated post-merger pricing.

In appraising the value of elasticity information gleaned from an econometric analysis of scanner data, is noteworthy that others, such as marketing professionals, also undertake similar analyses. For example, manufacturers of consumer products estimate systems of demand equations to help them determine optimal prices for their products. Clearly, scanner data, drawn from consumers' actual purchases, provides a wealth of information that can be used to describe and analyze consumer demand..

While the quantitative estimation of demand relationships can make substantial contributions to merger analysis, it is much like every other area of empirical economics, in that practitioners invariably are forced to confront and resolve a series of difficult econometric and conceptual issues. The purpose of this paper is to identify a number of econometric and conceptual issues that we believe researchers and practitioners should address in order to make the quantitative estimation of demand relationships using scanner data more applicable to merger review.

Briefly, we raise the following issues in this paper:

1. What is the best way to aggregate data across observational units and across time?

2. What are the consequences of choosing a particular functional form for an empirical demand curve?

3. Is it necessary to address the possible endogeneity of explanatory variables?

4. Is it possible to construct meaningful measures of the accuracy of predicted price changes?

5. Can one easily translate elasticities estimated with retail-level data into wholesale-level elasticities?

These are difficult questions, and we do not attempt to provide definitive answers to them. Our purpose instead is to provoke further discussion and research into these issues, with the ultimate goal of improving the quality of antitrust analysis.

II. DATA ISSUES

A. Scanner Data Features

The two leading providers of scanner data are A.C. Nielsen (Nielsen) and Information Resources Incorporated (IRI). Both firms provide a variety of retail information in a number of channels of distribution (supermarkets, drug stores, mass-merchandisers, and convenience stores) for various geographic regions throughout the U.S. The bases of these data sold by Nielsen and IRI are a sample of stores from which the data companies acquire all point-of-sale (POS) scanner data. The scanner data provides data on total revenue and total units sold by UPC code.[4] In addition, IRI and Nielsen collect a number of measures of price and of various measures of promotion for each retail outlet they sample, *e.g.*, a specific chain and store location, and a measure of distribution penetration.[5]

The data collected by IRI and Nielsen represent a sample of the retail outlets operating in the U.S., and both firms use different proprietary methods to project total sales. IRI and Nielsen cover some areas, and some distribution channels, better than others. Both IRI and Nielsen have very good coverage from supermarkets. There is significantly less coverage in the mass-merchandiser and convenience store channels. For products that have substantial sales outside the supermarket channel, the IRI and Nielsen data can present questions as to the representativeness of the data. However, to our knowledge, the data from IRI and Nielsen are the best available to study demand for these products.

Although the "raw" data contains each individual POS transaction, the data Nielsen and IRI sell to their clients typically consists of *aggregates* of total sales in dollars and units by brand and UPC code. To our knowledge, IRI and Nielsen rarely sell (aggregated) price and quantity information from individual stores. Instead, they typically aggregate the quantity and revenue data up to either the level of the chain within a specific geographic area, *e.g.*, Giant Foods in the Washington, DC metropolitan area, or, more

---

[4] UPC refers to Universal Product Code. A UPC corresponds to a precise package size/brand of a consumer product. For example, a UPC would refer to a 15 ounce package of General Mills Cheerios cereal. The 10 ounce box of Cheerios would be a separate UPC as would the 15 ounce box of Honey Nut Cheerios. Within a single product category, e.g. ready-to-eat cereal, there are literally thousands of different UPCs.

[5] A product's percentage of "All Commodity Volume" (typically referred to as ACV) is defined to be the ratio of the revenue of retailer outlets carrying a product in a given geographic area to the sales of all retailers in that geographic area. For example, a food product with a percent of ACV of 70% in the Washington, D.C. metro area would be carried by retailer food outlets that account for 70% of food revenues in Washington, D.C.

often, aggregate over all chains and stores within a geographic area for a given channel, e.g., revenue and quantity within the Washington, DC metropolitan area for all supermarkets.

IRI and Nielsen also collect data on shelf prices; however, there are potential measurement problems with this data. The most important problems likely result from discounts (e.g., coupons or club) received by some consumers but not observed (or only imperfectly observed) in the data. For example, if a consumer purchased Coke at $3.99 and used a $.50 coupon, the price would be recorded as $3.99. There is a similar problem for "club" or "loyalty card" purchases, which entitle a customer with a card to a substantial discount on promoted items. In some cases, the price is recorded as the most commonly occurring price (typically the price with a club card), in other times average revenue is recorded. An additional issue in both the IRI and Nielsen data results from the time interval over which data is collected. While both collect and report data weekly, different retailers change their prices on different days of the week, e.g. promotions at some retailers run Sunday to Saturday, while others run on a Thursday to Wednesday schedule. Thus, it is quite possible that the shelf price reported by IRI or Nielsen in a given week will only correspond to the actual shelf price for a portion of the reported week.

IRI and Nielsen collect three general measures of promotional activity that can be used in demand studies.[6] First, the firms create measures of advertising of specific items in a retailer's circular. Roughly speaking, an advertisement is coded as an "A" ad if it appears on the front or back cover of an advertising circular, a "B" ad if it appears inside the circular but has a graphical representation of the item, and a "C" ad if the item is

---

[6] Retailers engage in a number of non-price promotional activities (often supported in some way by manufacturers) that can dramatically affect sales at a retailer. For example, a case study by Progressive Grocer reported that sales of household cleansers increased 50% with a price cut and an advertisement, but increased by 1,900% when also given a display (see "The Real Power of Promotion" Progressive Grocer, page 39, December, 1992). Market researchers and economists too have found that, holding price constant, promotional activities by retailers can have large incremental effects on sales (Montgomery (1997), Hoch, Kim, Montgomery, and Rossi (1995), Abraham and Lodish (1993), and Katz and Shapiro (1986) are just a few examples of papers in the marketing literature which explicitly incorporate measures of promotion and advertising in their estimation of demand systems). As an example, a weekly period in which Coke was sold at a discount price of $2.99 is likely to have significantly fewer sales than a weekly period in which Coke was sold at $2.99 accompanied by significant promotional activity. Economic theory does not give explicit guidance as to how this activity should be empirically modeled. For example, does promotional activity change the amount consumers would be willing to pay at any given price, or does promotional activity change the consumer's price sensitivity? Given the empirical significance of advertising variables in marketing studies, it is likely the case that including information on advertising and promotion can improve the accuracy of demand studies used by antitrust economists.

simply mentioned in the circular. Second, IRI and Nielsen record what proportion of stores have in-store promotional displays for items, e.g., an end of aisle display or some type of free-standing display. Finally, the firms record whether or not a coupon was released in a geographic area, typically as a "free-standing-insert" of the type found in the Saturday or Sunday edition of a newspaper. Including these measures of promotion can significantly enhance the accuracy of a demand study. However, if (as is typically the case) the data is aggregated across retailers, the aggregation to some extent "masks" the interactive effect between price promotions and other forms of promotions. For example, knowing that 50% of the retailers (by some measure of total sales) had an end aisle display does not allow us to match the price those stores set, since the measure of price is an average across the "market."

Because many antitrust practitioners have a vague notion of what exactly scanner data is, we believe it is beneficial to explicitly describe the data used by the FTC in a recent court case. In *FTC v. Swedish Match,* both the Commission and respondents presented estimates of the own-price elasticity for loose-leaf chewing tobacco based on monthly data from all retail channels (supermarkets, drug stores, convenience stores, and mass-merchandisers) and aggregated across regions within a state. The data used by the FTC and Swedish Match in the studies presented to the Court was aggregated to the category level; that is, all UPCs of each brand (e.g, Red Man, Levi-Garret, or Beechnut Chewing Tobacco) were aggregated into a single number for loose leaf chewing tobacco. The data was also aggregated over: the time unit (from weekly to monthly), geography (all retailers within a state), retail channels (supermarkets, drug stores, mass merchandisers, convenience stores), retailers, brands, and UPC's within the brand (package sizes). An example of an individual data point would be total dollar and unit sales of (all brands of) loose leaf chewing tobacco sold in Illinois in all measured retail channels for March, 1999. Below we discuss the potential problems associated with the various types of data aggregation that are required to conduct an econometric analysis with scanner data.

B. General Aggregation Issues

One of the most significant issues in using scanner data to estimate demand estimates is the nature and extent of data aggregation. As discussed above, the data that is available is already aggregated across time (*e.g.*, weekly), and also typically aggregated across retailers, often in a large geographic area. In addition, the researcher generally finds it necessary to undertake additional aggregations, to make the estimation tractable. For example, estimating demand for each individual size or variation of a given consumer product is generally not practical, and attempting to do so would often lead to imprecise parameter estimates. Unfortunately, aggregating the data requires the researcher to make assumptions which may have important effects on the parameter estimates. In this section of the paper we describe three major types of aggregation that in our experience can impact the demand estimates.

1. Channel Aggregation

Most consumer products are sold in a number of different channels, however, it is often the case that some channels of distribution are more important for a given product than others. For example, many food products are sold almost exclusively through supermarkets, e.g., canned soup, salad dressing, and cake mix. In these cases, simply using data from the supermarket channel should be sufficient to describe the demand system for the products. Other product categories have large sales of products through multiple channels, e.g., soft drinks and snack food are sold in significant quantities through convenience stores, grocery stores and mass-merchandisers.

When consumers purchase the same consumer products through different channels, aggregation of sales and unit data across channels could lead to different elasticity estimates than if the elasticities were estimated separately by channel for at least two reasons. First, consumers choose to shop in different channels for different reasons. For example, consumers shopping at a convenience store likely have less elastic demand for products than those shopping at a supermarket. One would expect that consumers' beer purchases through convenience stores would be less sensitive to price than purchases through grocery stores. The same pattern likely holds when comparing products carried by one channel more as a convenience (such as motor oil at a supermarket) to retailers that specialize in selling those products (such as motor oil through a mass-merchandiser).

Second, the mix of package sizes of a given product/brand (e.g., *Pepsi Cola*) sold through different channels also varies significantly. For example, the share of single serve packages of cola (20 ounce bottles or 12 ounce cans) sold through convenience stores is much larger than that sold through supermarkets. If sales and revenue are calculated at the brand level (Pepsi) as opposed to the UPC level (20 ounce bottle of Pepsi, 2 liter bottle of Pepsi, 12 pack of Pepsi), then measures of revenue and sales from different channels will not be comparable because of differences in product mix across channels. In our experience, we have found for markets where substantial sales of the product occur in different retail channels of distribution, that the estimated demand elasticities can be quite different when estimated separately by channel.

2. Aggregation Over Time

In estimating demand systems for consumer products, staff often have access to weekly scanner data from supermarkets. There are two primary advantages to using weekly data as opposed to a more aggregated form (e.g., monthly or quarterly). First, because grocery stores tend to change their prices weekly (promotions typically last one or two weeks), weekly data most accurately relate consumer prices to their corresponding purchases. Second, the use of weekly data gives the researcher many more observations which increase the precision of elasticity estimates. On the other hand, for the purpose for which we perform these estimations, *i.e.*, getting information about demand at the *manufacturer* level, the frequency of scanner data presents other problems. Unlike retailers, manufacturers do not change their wholesale prices on a weekly basis.[7]

Time aggregation also relates to another problem that we will discuss further below -- purchasing for inventory. Using weekly or even monthly data may overestimate elasticities because consumers often buy large quantities of items which are on sale and take them into household inventories; that is, the elasticities being measured are really short run purchasing elasticities not the consumption elasticities which are relevant for antitrust analysis. Economics and marketing researchers both find that inventory effects can be important.[8] Because the goal of antitrust analysis is to measure the effects on consumer demand of permanent changes in price, it is important to measure elasticities that measure changes in consumer consumption due to changes in price. If inventory effects are important (this is likely to be the case if the predominate source of price variation are the sales which generate inventory effects), the estimated elasticities will likely be too large and should only serve as an upper bound for the demand elasticities for the purposes of antitrust analysis.

Empirically, we have found that elasticity estimated using weekly data are often larger than those estimated using monthly data.

3. Aggregation Across Product Sizes and Varieties

Many types of consumer products are sold in different package sizes, with the price per unit of weight or volume generally declining with package size. Further, it is sometimes the case that different package sizes are sold more through some channels of distribution than others. For example, mass-merchandisers focus more on selling large package sizes (either through better pricing or enhanced in-store promotion and display), while convenience stores typically sell a product's small package sizes.

As a practical matter, when estimating a demand system, a researcher is required to make some aggregation choices to minimize the number of parameters to be estimated. In some markets aggregation across package sizes is not very important because most sales are made through one package size, e.g. shaving cream, motor oil, and shampoo. However, in other markets significant volume is sold through multiple package sizes, e.g., pet food, ready-to-eat cereal, and soda. Further, substitution between package sizes within a brand is often empirically important. In our merger investigations, we have seen

---

[7] Although manufacturers may offer discounts to retailers during promotions during discrete time periods, e.g. a month, which may be viewed as a temporary discount on the wholesale price.

[8] Pesendorfer (2002) develops a model of intertemporal price discrimination and finds evidence that lagged prices affect the current level of demand (consistent with consumer inventory behavior). Hosken and Reiffen (1999) also develop a model of intertemporal price discrimination and discuss the effects of such a model on estimating demand systems. Hendal and Nevo (2001) provide empirical evidence on the importance of inventory effects.

firms conduct sophisticated studies trying to determine how much substitution will take place between different package sizes of their own brands. In terms of estimating demand systems, we have observed that different aggregation rules (e.g., average price per pound, the creation of a price index, or estimating elasticities separately by package size) can lead to very different estimated demand elasticities. The fixes to this problem are not obvious or easy to undertake.[9]

C. Price Specification and Aggregation

The scanner data that is typically used in estimating demand curves is aggregated over some geographic area, e.g., a census region, state, or metro area, and across retailers, by channel, in that area. Obviously, if independent pricing decisions are made by stores within the geographic areas the price and quantity observed in the data (typically price defined as average revenue, and units defined as the sum of all units in the area) will not correspond to the prices charged (quantities sold) by any individual firm. There are two distinct types of problems that result from aggregation across retailers. The first comes from the observation that the aggregate price, as measured by average revenue, and aggregate output will not correspond to a point on the aggregate demand curve because average revenue is a non-linear function of each retailer's average revenue. The second set of problems are the result of un-modeled phenomena (e.g., sales, promotion, and other forms of retail competition) that cause consumers to not face the aggregate price as measured by average revenue. As discussed in more detail below, the second set of problems leads to more difficult questions on how to appropriately use price and quantity data to correctly estimate elasticities which manufacturers are likely to face.

A simple example can demonstrate how measuring price as average revenue can lead to biased elasticity estimates when demand curves are linear demand. Assume that there are three retailers operating in a geographic area, and, for simplicity, assume that the firms do not compete with one another because they are in separate geographic markets. The price and quantity data that the researcher observes is aggregated from the three firms. To be explicit assume that:

Firm 1's demand curve is: $Q = 1000 - 5*P$
Firm 2's demand curve is: $Q = 1000 - 8*P$
Firm 3's demand curve is: $Q = 1000 - 10*P$.

The aggregate demand firm for the region will be:

$Q = 3000 - 23*P$.

---

[9] In principal, one could attempt to formally incorporate the non-linear budget set into the econometric model, e.g., Reiss and White (2001). However, in the time required to estimate a demand system in a merger investigation this approach is not currently feasible. Instead, the approach BE has taken is to check the robustness of our results to different measures of price.

When we estimate a demand curve, we estimate a relationship like

$Q = A - B*P$,

where A and B are parameters to be estimated, and we use a single measure of price (aggregated in some manner; *e.g.*, average revenue)

If each firm charges the same price at every point in time, we can correctly estimate the demand curve using average revenue as the measure of price. However if the three firms charge different prices at the same point in time, then the estimated aggregate demand curve will not correspond to the true aggregate demand curve.

To illustrate the misspecification we conduct a simple simulation with 1500 price (and corresponding quantity) draws for each firm where firms 1, 2, and 3 set prices independently (but where prices were drawn from the same distribution), and find that the least squares estimate of the demand curve using the average unit price as the measure of price is: $Q = 2687 - 19.3*P$, which represents a significant underestimate of the true slope of the demand curve (see Figure 1 which presents a plot of the average price and total quantity data).[10]

---

[10] In the simulation we model each retailer as randomly drawing prices from a uniform distribution with prices between 0 and 100.

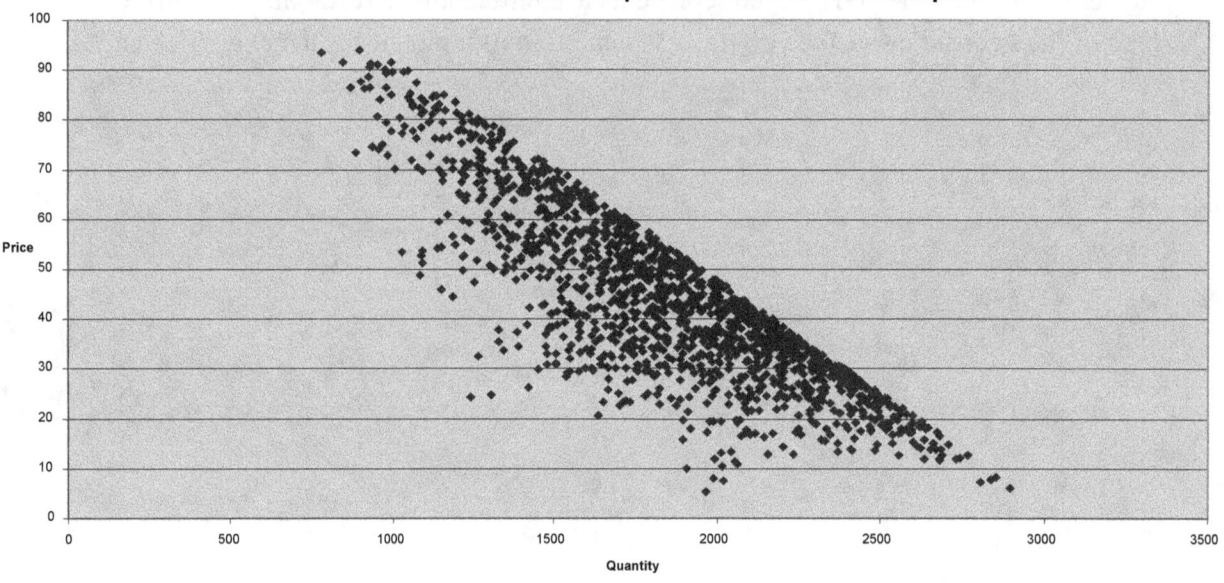
Figure 1: Average Price and Total Quantity, Aggregate Three Demand Curves with Different Slopes but the Same Intercept

This example shows that even though each individual demand curve is linear, the relationship between aggregate quantity and market-level average revenue is not. Thus, estimating an aggregate demand curve using a similarly aggregated average price measure can provide misleading inferences about the aggregate demand sensitivity.[11, 12]

Most of the scanner data used in estimating demand curves combines price and quantity data across retailers within a broad geographic area, such as a metro area. As described above, because retailers charge different prices, the price and quantity data aggregated across retailers do not represent the prices faced by any consumer.[13] A further problem arises because of non-price competition that varies across retailers within a market at a

---

[11] This example is intended merely to demonstrate the potential bias resulting from aggregation. However, strictly speaking, the model presented above is not internally consistent. An aggregate demand curve is only well defined if the products being aggregated are homogeneous. Presumably, the fact that the different firms charge different prices violates the homogeneity assumption. However, since we know that different retailers in different areas charge very different prices at the same time (see Hosken and Reiffen, 1999), the example indicates that the aggregation across markets can "matter," and that the aggregation choices typically made by researchers could be problematic.

[12] The problems associated with aggregating demand curves across consumers (or equivalently collections of consumers) has been well known for some time and was the subject of much research on demand estimation (Gorman's (1959) work was some of the first to deal with these issues. Deaton and Muellbauer's (1980) book *Economics and Consumer Behavior* provides an excellent description of the problems of aggregation and the estimation of demand systems). However, this earlier literature did not address the problems created by consumer paying different prices. The problem of price aggregation in analysis of scanner data is discussed in Scheffman (1992). As a practical matter, not much can be done to solve this problem other than trying to get access to more disaggregated data or making very specific assumptions about the structure of demand (e.g., AIDS).

[13] Recall that the raw data consist of innumerable individual transactions that may differ during the reporting period in the prices paid by consumers. For example, if the reported data, as is typically the case, aggregates across supermarkets during the period, the reported aggregated data would sum up transactions at Chain X selling the particular UPC code at $1 with transactions at Chain Y at $1.30. The typical *estimate* of price would be average revenue, *i.e.*, total sales divided by total units. Clearly, this measure does not capture the variability in prices across stores. For example, if sales were split evenly between Chain X and Chain Y, the *estimate* of price would be $1.15. But this would be the same measure of price if both X and Y had prices of $1.15 during the reporting period. As will be discussed below, this may present significant issues in attempting to estimate consumer (retail-level) demand.

point in time. For example, it is well known that advertisements in circulars and in-store promotional activity (e.g., end of aisle displays) have large effects on unit sales.[14]

If a given chain charges approximately the same prices and offers similar promotions within a metro area, chain-specific data should accurately reflect the price and non-price attributes facing consumers in a given week. IRI and Nielsen do maintain these data; however, they have rarely been used in antitrust investigations.

While retailer-specific data reduce the problem of measurement error, the demand parameters estimated from retailer-specific data do not necessarily correspond to the parameters of interest to antitrust economists. The goal of the demand study is to determine the demand elasticities facing the manufacturer, *not* its retailers. As a matter of simple economic theory, we know that the demand curve facing competing retailers in a region will be more elastic than the aggregate demand curve for the entire market. For example, assume that there is a highly perishable product for which consumer demands are virtually completely inelastic (e.g., milk), and also that some fraction of consumers are loyal to shopping at their favorite store, while others shop at the store with the lowest milk price. Assume further that supermarket chains compete for the non-loyal customers by offering milk at discounted prices (in some kind of mixed-price equilibrium).[15] In the data, when a chain happens to have the lowest price for milk in a given week it will experience a surge in sales (because it captures all of the non-loyal consumers), while the total quantity of milk sold in the market is unchanged. Thus, the demand elasticity for milk estimated using chain data will be large, while the market level elasticity (correctly measured using market level data) is zero.

Whether the analysis should use chain-specific or market-specific data will depend on the question being asked. As described above, if the analyst is trying to infer the market level demand for a product and consumers are likely to change retailers to purchase that product given small changes in that product's price, then chain-specific data may not yield good elasticity estimates. However, if consumers are unlikely to change retailers to purchase a product at a promoted price, then market/chain specific data is probably preferable to market-level data aggregated over chains.

III. Functional Forms in Demand Estimation and Merger Simulation

A. Introduction

Empirical estimation of market-level demand equations requires the analyst to specify functional form for the equation prior to estimation. A number of criteria must be considered in making this choice. Most researchers wish to preserve "flexibility" (*i.e.,* they wish to avoid predetermining the pattern of substitution possibilities among the

---

[14] Meaning, in a regression setting, holding price constant, the presence of advertising or in-store displays increases unit sales significantly.

[15] See Varian (1980) for an example of such a model.

commodities being analyzed by the particular choice of functional form) – or to put it more simply, they want to allow the data to tell them whether two goods are substitutes, and if so, whether they are close or distant substitutes).

The problem researchers face is that "flexibility" is expensive, in the sense that a great deal of data is required to estimate demand equations that have this property. If a researcher is estimating the demand relationships among, say, five different products, he or she must estimate 25 own- and cross-price elasticities. If there are 10 products, the number of price elasticities (own and cross) that must be estimated increases to 100. Given that the typical antitrust economist usually only has access to several years of data, it can become difficult to estimate with acceptable precision the demand elasticities for even a modest number of products.[16] And, as these demand elasticities are the critical inputs into calculating the predicted post-merger price change, imprecision in the former naturally translates into imprecision in the latter.

In what follows, we briefly review and summarize the current state of knowledge about the implications of choosing particular functional forms.

---

[16] In Bresnahan (1987) there were 100 different auto models analyzed, yielding 10,000 elasticities.

B. Choosing Functional Forms

Here we will focus principally on the functional forms that have experienced widespread use in merger simulations; readers seeking a more general discussion are referred to Deaton and Muellbauer (1980).

In estimating demand at retail, the researcher must choose the mathematical formula (functional form) that expresses the demand relationship. The statistical estimation, itself, does not "choose" the functional form. In theory, there is a "true" functional form that generates the purchase data, and of course it is important that the functional form chosen for estimation approximates the "true" functional form. As a matter of practice, assessing the validity of the functional form chosen for estimation is done through various statistical tests and testing alternative functional forms.

In the typical antitrust setting in which demand estimation and merger simulation occurs, the researcher will have data for a number of different cities (*e.g.*, 30 of the largest cities in the U.S.). For each product (or brand) analyzed, the dataset will consist of the number of units sold in some particular time period (*e.g.*, a week), a measure of the price that prevailed during that period,[17] and also measures of promotional activity for each product. Using standard econometric techniques,[18] the researcher will estimate a statistical relationship between the quantity of the good purchased and the price and promotional activities and other determinants of demand (such as the size of the market).

Choice of functional form can have major implications for the magnitude of predicted prices. Crooke *et al.* (1999) show that different functional forms can produce substantially differing predictions about post-merger equilibria. For example, if the researcher assumes that the demand functions exhibit constant elasticities, the predicted post-merger price increases will be much larger than if linear or logit demands are assumed.

One possible functional form is the linear demand system. One major advantage to the linear demand system is that it makes computation of the merger's competitive effects relatively easy (see Werden (1996) for details). There are numerous drawbacks to the linear demand system. First, there is no guarantee that the estimated parameters will have the "right" sign. If the different brands are substitutes, then the cross-price terms should be positive, in order to yield a positive cross-elasticity. However, it is frequently the case in applied work that the estimated cross-price coefficients will be negative, which calls into question the validity of the empirical exercise.

---

[17] As discussed above, the measure of "price" typically used is average revenue (= $(p*q)/q$), which often will not give an accurate measure of the prices actually faced by consumers during that week. For purposes of the present discussion, however, we will ignore this issue.

[18] We defer to Section III the economic and econometric issues associated with endogeneity of the price and promotion variables.

A second, more subtle problem is identified by Crooke *et al.* (1999), who found that simulations conducted with linear demand systems sometimes can yield *negative* predicted quantities.

An alternative to linear demand systems is the *log-linear* (*i.e.,* constant elasticity) demand function. This system is estimated by regressing the natural logarithms of the quantity variables on the natural logarithms of the price and demand-shifting variables. The appeal of the constant elasticity system is that the regression coefficients are the elasticities – no further computations are required. There are several disadvantages to this functional form. First, the "adding-up" restriction of demand theory (i.e., the requirement that expenditure shares sum to unity) cannot be satisfied by the constant elasticity demand system (Deaton and Muellbauer, 1980, p. 17). Second, many researchers prefer to allow demand elasticities to vary as prices and quantities vary (*e.g.,* as in the linear, logit, and AIDS demand systems, where demand becomes more elastic as one moves up the demand curve). If the true demand system is not constant elasticity, yet the researcher assumes otherwise for the purpose of merger simulation, the resulting predicted price increases can substantially overstate the likely price effects (Crooke *et al.* (1999)). A third disadvantage is that, depending on the values taken on by the elasticities, merger simulations may lead to a situation in which post-merger equilibrium does not always exist (Crooke *et al.* 1999). Last, the log-linear system, like the linear system, cannot guarantee that the parameters have the "right" signs.

The disadvantages of the linear and log-linear systems are sufficiently large that many researchers now use alternative functional forms in merger analysis.[19] One popular choice is the *Almost Ideal Demand System* (popularly termed the "AIDS" model), first proposed by Deaton and Muellbauer (1980), and advocated by Hausman *et al.* (1994) as a basis for empirical merger analysis. In the AIDS model, expenditure shares of each product are regressed on the logarithms of the prices of the different goods and the log of total expenditure (deflated by a price index). The principal disadvantages are that, like other functional forms (*e.g.,* linear), it requires the estimation of a large number of parameters, and it does not guarantee (at least without further restrictions) that cross-elasticities have the "right" signs. Additionally, although AIDS allows elasticities to adjust as equilibrium prices and quantities vary, it restricts somewhat the way these adjustments take place; consequently, the predictions of models estimated using the AIDS specification do not vary greatly from those estimated under an assumption of constant elasticities (Crooke *et al.* (1999, Table III)).

The burden of estimating a large number of parameters can be addressed by employing functional forms that have fewer free parameters. Werden and Froeb (1994) and Werden *et al.* (1996) have advocated the use of the logit model. The appeal of the logit model is found in its analytical tractability and its relatively modest data requirements. The logit model assumes that consumers make a discrete choice from a set of (exhaustive) alternatives. For example, if the good being analyzed is breakfast cereals, it is assumed

---

[19] It is of interest to note, however, that market researchers who develop estimates of elasticities for grocery manufacturers often do use linear or log linear models.

that the consumer chooses the brand of cereal yielding the highest utility (he also has the alternative of choosing "none of the above," which is referred to as the "outside good."). With aggregate share data, the parameters of a simple logit model can be estimated as follows:

$$\log(S_j/S_O) = \beta^* x_j + \alpha^* p_j + \gamma^* \log(S_{j|g}) + \varepsilon_j$$

Here, S_j is the market share of product "j"; S_O is the share of the "outside good;" x_j are characteristics of good "j"; p_j is the price of good "j"; and $S_{j|g}$ is the market share of product "j" within segment "g". To illustrate with an example, Irwin and Pavcnik (2001) analyze the competition between Boeing and Airbus within the market segment consisting of wide-bodied aircraft. Here, the typical S_j is the share (out of total aircraft, narrow and wide-bodied) of a particular plane, such as the Airbus A-320; S_O is the share of all narrow-bodied aircraft; $S_{j|g}$ is the share of the A-320 in the *wide-bodied* segment; the x_j are the observable (to the econometrician) characteristics of the A-320; and p_j is its price. Once the parameters α, β, and γ are estimated, own- and cross-price elasticities can be easily computed.

The major analytical criticism of the logit model is that it embodies the restrictive assumption of the Independence of Irrelevant Alternatives.[20] In the context of logit models of demand, the IIA property implies that if the price of one good increases, consumers switch to other goods in proportion to the latter's market shares. This is a highly restrictive assumption that clearly will not be valid in many instances.[21]

To avoid the highly restrictive pattern of cross-elasticities embodied in the simple logit model, but at the same time preserving its parsimony in terms of parameters requiring estimation, researchers have developed alternative models of demand that not only allow for much greater flexibility in substitution patterns, but which also allow the researcher to take into account heterogeneous consumer preferences and the likely endogeneity of product prices. Berry, Levinsohn, and Pakes (*see* Berry (1994); Berry, Levinsohn, and

---

[20] Hausman and Leonard (1997, p. 322) note that "[a]s has been known for many years, the logit demand model makes the IIA assumption, which implicitly restricts the demand structure by constraining the pattern of demand structure by constraining the pattern of demand substitution between products. Indeed, it has been known for over twenty years that the logit demand system makes the assumption of *identical* cross-price elasticities for all products with respect to a given product . . . restricting the demand substitution patterns [in this way] would seem to defeat the purpose of performing unilateral effects analysis."

[21] There is another possible empirical problem with the logit specification. Many studies of household behavior indicate that the same household often regularly purchases multiple brands. (Recall that the purchasing unit is probably best viewed as the household, with the grocery shopper(s) making purchases on behalf of all the household members).

Pakes (1995); Nevo (2000)) have proposed a random coefficients logit model that assumes that products can be viewed as bundles of characteristics (*e.g.,* automobiles might be characterized by horsepower, passenger space, and air conditioning). Accordingly, their empirical model is specified in terms of the demand for these characteristics, which are far fewer in number than the number of products (or brands) that compete in the market at any given time. The data required to estimate the random coefficients logit model may not always be particularly demanding – in some cases, they can be estimated with market-level price and quantity data, data on product characteristics, and information on the distribution of consumer attributes (*e.g.,* income, education) – but the estimation procedure itself is complex and time-consuming. The full details of the BLP approach are too complex to be presented in detail here. Nevo (2000) provides an excellent summary.

IV. Estimation Issues

A. Endogeneity

For statistical analysis of sample data to produce "reliable" results -- that is, results that accurately convey information about the underlying population -- certain conditions must hold. The data we use in the estimation is the product of both demand-side and supply-side factors. Care must be taken to insure that what is actually being estimated is the demand relationship rather than some combination of demand and supply. One important issue is whether explanatory variables in the demand relationship (e.g., price) are correlated with "disturbances" that shift the demand relationship. For example, if stores change prices during the period of data reporting in response to "unexpected" changes in the volume of purchases, we would say that prices are "endogenous," as opposed to a situation in which stores set their prices in advance of the data period and do not change prices during the data period, despite occasional unexpected changes in the volume of sales.

Even if prices (or other explanatory variables, such as promotions variables) are endogenous, there are statistical methods that, in principle, can produce reliable estimates. Although there a number of approaches to addressing the problem of endogeneity, perhaps the most commonly used method is some variant of what is known as "instrumental variables" estimation. An instrumental variable is some variable that the researcher believes is correlated with the explanatory variable of interest (here, price) but uncorrelated with the unobserved "disturbances" that shift the demand curve. Good candidates for instrumental variables would be the prices of inputs used in the production of the product, since they are likely to be correlated with the supply curve (at retail) but not disturbances that shift the demand curve. Such data series are generally termed "costs shifters."

In the context of demand estimation with scanner data, however, it is usually difficult to find enough cost shifters, since the analyst would need as many different costs shifters are there are prices in the demand system. One commonly used estimation strategy is that proposed by Hausman *et al.* (1994) and Hausman (1997).[22] To use this approach, the analyst assembles data on prices and quantities for a number of different cities for a given time period. Under the assumption that unobserved shocks to product costs affect all cities equally (*i.e.*, there are no city-specific cost shocks) but that there are city-specific demand shocks (and not nationwide demand shocks), the prices in other cities can serve as valid instruments for the price in any particular city (*i.e.*, the prices of soft drinks in (say) Detroit, Minneapolis, and Denver can serve as instruments for the price of soft drinks in Chicago).

The legitimacy of this proposed solution to the endogeneity problem is controversial. Bresnahan (1997a, 1997b), for example, contested its validity in the context of ready-to-eat cereals demand estimation. Bresnahan argues (1997a, pp. 241-2) that if, for example, there are national advertising campaigns whose effectiveness is imperfectly measured by the econometrician, there will be a national component to the demand disturbance, which will in turn invalidate the restrictions necessary for implementation of the Hausman method. If Bresnahan's criticism is correct, the resulting estimates of the relationship between price and quantity will be biased towards zero (Bresnahan (1997, pp. 241-2)). Nevo (2000, pp. 535-36) makes a similar point.

It can be argued that endogeneity of prices is not a major issue in the econometric estimation of retail demand functions using supermarket scanner data. For example, Hausman (1997, 219-20) has argued that if supermarkets do not adjust weekly prices to equilibrate demand and supply, and if supply curves are flat, prices can be treated as econometrically predetermined, thus obviating the need for instrumental variables estimation procedures. The validity of this reasoning also has been questioned. Bresnahan (1997a, p. 241) has argued that this reasoning assumes that the (common) demand shocks (*e.g.*, from national ad campaigns) cannot be foreseen when retail prices are set, an assumption that he regards as unlikely. Bresnahan also argues that short-run retailer supply curves may be upward-sloping, rather than flat, because of retailer market power or inventory-adjustment costs.

B. Inference

Statistical inference – drawing inferences about a population from information contained in a sample drawn from that population – requires the analyst to carry out two tasks: first, he must compute the statistic of interest (e.g., the sample mean); and second, he must compute some measure of the accuracy of that statistic as an estimate of the corresponding population value (i.e., the population mean). Unless the analyst has this second piece of information, he has no idea whether his estimate of the truth is likely to be fairly close, or substantially off the mark. As recently stated by Koenker and Hallock

---

[22] The method used in Hausman et al. (1994) and Hausman (1997) was derived by Hausman and Taylor (1981). The Hausman-Taylor article proposes an instrumental variables method for estimating the coefficients on time-invariant characteristics in a panel data setting.

(2001, p. 153), "[i]t is a basic principle of sound econometrics that *every serious estimate deserves a reliable assessment of precision,*" [emphasis original].

Suppose, for example, that the analyst wished to know the average retail price of a 1-litre bottle of Coca-Cola sold in the Washington, D.C. metro area. He could visit 50 retail locations, record the price at each location, and compute the mean for the sample. Using standard statistical techniques, he could compute the estimated variance of the sample mean, and construct a confidence interval, which would give a sense of how precisely the sample mean likely approximates the true population mean (*i.e.,* the mean that would be computed if the researcher visited *every* retail location where Coke is sold).

This basic approach to gauging the accuracy of a sample statistic extends in a straightforward manner to more complicated settings, such as estimating a set of linear regression coefficients – or linear functions of these coefficients – and their associated variances. The formulas for carrying out these computations can be found in every econometrics text, and standard econometric software packages calculate them effortlessly. But matters quickly become analytically and computationally difficult if the researcher is interested in nonlinear functions of the regression coefficients. In these circumstances, the analyst must rely on alternative methods for approximating the variances. These methods may or may not convey useful information about the true variance, and may prove computationally difficult to carry out.

A simple example may help illustrate. Suppose we are estimating a simple regression equation using ordinary least squares

$$y = \beta_0 + \beta_1 X + \varepsilon$$
$$\equiv X\beta + \varepsilon$$
$$E[\varepsilon] = 0;$$
$$V[\varepsilon] = \sigma^2 I$$

If we have N observations on y and x, the OLS estimate of β_1 (denoted as $\underline{b}$ (= $[b_0\ b_1]'$) is $(X'X)^{-1}X'y$, and its variance (Σ) equals $\sigma^2(X'X)^{-1}$. Since the parameter is unknown, it must be replaced with its estimate s^2 (= $\underline{e}'\underline{e}/(n-1)$, where $\underline{e} = \underline{y} - X\underline{b}$). Thus armed with the estimated regression coefficients ($\underline{b}$) and their estimated variances s^2_b [$s^2(X'X)^{-1}$], the analyst can proceed to test hypotheses about the true regression parameters. If the analyst is prepared to assume that β_1 is distributed multivariate normal, then in small samples linear functions of $\underline{b}$ and its estimated standard error (s_b) will have a t-distribution. If the distribution of β_1 is unknown, then (provided the sample is sufficiently large) the analyst can invoke the asymptotic (large sample) properties of the least squares estimator and use the normal distribution to test hypotheses about β_1. A common hypothesis test is whether $\beta_1 = 0$; the test statistic is b_1/s_b, and the "critical values" are obtained (depending on the sample size) from the tabulated values of the t- or standard normal distributions.

Suppose now that the analyst is not interested in testing hypotheses about regression parameter β_1, but is instead interested in the elasticity of y with respect to x, defined as $\eta = \beta_1(\bar{x}/\bar{y})$. In empirical applications, it is common to calculate this elasticity by using the estimated parameter (b_1) and the sample means for $\bar{x}$ and $\bar{y}$. While it is easy to compute this estimated elasticity, it is not readily apparent how to compute its standard error, a necessary ingredient for hypothesis testing, nor is it obvious what the distribution of $\tilde{\eta}$ will be, even if the small sample distribution of b_1 is known.

One approach, known as the "delta method" (see Greene (1997), p. 280; Goldberger (1991), p. 102), uses asymptotic distribution theory to show that if $\underline{b} \sim N(\underline{\beta}, \Sigma)$, then asymptotically f($\underline{b}$) is distributed normally with mean f($\underline{\beta}$) and variance f'($\underline{b}$)V($\underline{b}$)f'($\underline{b}$)'.

There are two possible problems with the use of the delta method. First, it is valid only asymptotically; if the sample is insufficiently large, one cannot necessarily infer that the functions of $\underline{b}$ are normally distributed, and the asymptotic standard errors may provide a poor approximation of the standard errors in small samples. Second, and perhaps more important in the context of demand estimation, the functions that researchers are interested in (own- and cross-elasticities) are highly complex nonlinear functions of the regression parameters, which is a particular problem when the researcher uses a functional form such as the Almost Ideal Demand System (AIDS; see Green and Alston (1990)). And researchers are typically not interested in the elasticities themselves, but rather in functions of those elasticities (e.g., to compute predicted post-merger prices). It becomes computationally burdensome to calculate the variance matrix of the elasticities. Moreover, the delta method is based on the fact that the linear approximation to a function, and the function itself, has the same asymptotic distribution at a particular point. As one moves away from this point – as one might, for example, when simulating the effects of a merger – the asymptotic equivalence of these two distributions might no longer hold. Perhaps for these reasons, it is uncommon for researchers to provide estimated standard errors of the predicted price effects of mergers.

An alternative approach to computing standard errors for nonlinear functions is the "bootstrap" method (see Efron and Tibshirani (1993); Brownstone and Valletta (2001) provide a nontechnical discussion). The statistical theory behind the bootstrap is complex and will not be discussed here. Instead, we will describe its mechanics and comment on its utility in the particular application of merger simulation. Return to our example of computing the average price for a 1-litre bottle of Coke, with a sample of 50 prices. One could compute the sample mean and variance using the standard formulas found in any statistics textbook, and use these numbers to carry out tests of hypotheses about the mean price, to construct confidence intervals, etc. The alternative method for computing the variance is to use the bootstrap. For example, a confidence interval can by calculated by drawing a large number (e.g., 10,000) of "bootstrap samples" of size 50 (sampling is done with replacement) and computing the mean for each of these samples. The .025 and .975 percentiles of the distribution of the bootstrap sample means can then be used as the boundaries of the 95 percent confidence interval on the mean.

Why use the bootstrap? The bootstrap's appeal derives from (1) under fairly general conditions, the bootstrap approximations of the sampling distribution are at least as accurate – and under some conditions, more accurate – than the distributions obtained from asymptotic approximations; and (2) the bootstrap is relatively easy to implement.

One of the difficulties in using the bootstrap in the context of demand estimation is that the data are typically in the form of a "panel" – this is, time series-cross section data (*e.g.*, 3 years of monthly data on 50 cities). Because there may be serial correlation among the disturbances in the data, the normal bootstrap technique of random sampling from the data will be inappropriate. One possible solution to this problem would be to transform the data using standard procedures for autocorrelation (*e.g.*, the Cochrane-Orcutt procedure, suitably modified for panel data; *see* Green (1997), pp. 638-39) so that the variance matrix of the transformed disturbances no longer exhibit autocorrelation, and then carry out the bootstrap operations on the transformed data. Capps, Church, and Love (2001) propose an alternative method, based on a method originally developed by Freedman and Peters (1984).

V. Using Retail Price Data to Analyze Mergers of Manufacturers

A. Overview

The widespread availability of retail scanner data has made it possible to estimate demand systems and use the estimates to draw inferences about the potential effects of a merger. Most of the mergers that come before the agencies, however, occur at the manufacturer level, one or two stages upstream from retail pricing, which is determined at the retail level. An issue that is almost always ignored in the demand analyses that come before the agencies is the relationship between the demand elasticities estimated from *retail* data and the effects of a merger among *upstream* producers.[23]

We discuss two of issues here that we think deserve more attention. First, the own- and cross-elasticities of demand facing retailers are generally not the same as the own- and cross elasticities facing upstream wholesalers and manufacturers. Specific assumptions or analysis beyond that which is typically done is required to determine the demand elasticities facing upstream firms from estimates of retail elasticities.

Second, competition between upstream firms often takes place through more complicated contracts than the competition between producers of most final goods. The "prices" manufacturers charge retailers are often more complex than linear (i.e., per-unit) wholesale prices. They often include fixed fees of various types, quantity discounts, minimum or maximum purchase commitments, etc. In practice, payments between manufacturers and retailers are often broken into two components --- "list" prices and trade promotions. The list price is the unit price adjusted for any standard discounts and allowances, such as volume, prompt payment, etc. Trade promotions are various forms

---

[23] This is discussed Scheffman (1992) and in Scheffman and Spiller (1996). *See*, also, Steiner (1973, 1993, 2001).

of reductions from the list price and/or net payments from the manufacturer in various forms for features, displays, promotions, more favorable shelf space, etc. All of these factors can give rise to "nonlinear" payments (i.e., payments that are not made on a per-unit basis) between the manufacturer and the retailer, and this may have important implications for the analysis of a merger. In the next two subsections, we discuss these issues in more detail.[24]

B. Derived Demand Elasticities

When a manufacturer sells a product through retailers, the demand for its product is the quantity that retailers purchase to resell to final consumers. The quantity that retailers purchase depends on how profitable they think the product will be, which in turn depends (in part) on the "final demand" for the product from consumers. The demand facing the manufacturer is called a "derived demand" because it is "derived" from retailers' purchasing decisions, which are governed in part by the final demand for the product. The elasticities (own and cross) that are relevant for the manufacturer's pricing decision are the elasticities of the derived demand for its product.

It is well known that the elasticities of the derived demand facing manufacturers are generally not the same as the elasticities of the final demand estimated at the retail level. In general, the relationship depends on the form of the retail demand functions, the cost conditions of retailers, and the nature of retailer competition. Since we are often interested in the elasticities of derived demand, either for defining markets or for simulating manufacturer mergers, it is important to understand the nature of this relationship in specific environments.

A small amount of formal structure is useful. Suppose that the product in question is widgets, which a manufacturer sells to retailers for resale to final consumers. Denote the retail price for widgets as p and the wholesale price that retailers pay the manufacturer for

---

[24] A third issue that we do not discuss here is that the terms of exchange between manufacturers and retailers are determined through bargaining more often than the prices of final goods. Bargaining can have implications for the effects of mergers because a merger may change the bargaining positions (or "bargaining power") of the merging parties relative to firms on the other side of the market. See Horn and Wolinsky (1988), who examine the incentives for mergers between independent upstream firms (firms that do not compete with each other) and competing downstream firms when wholesale prices are negotiated. We are not aware of any literature on the effects of horizontal mergers between competing upstream manufacturers when wholesale prices are determined through bargaining.

each widget as w. The elasticity of the derived demand for the manufacturer's widgets can be written as[25]

$$E_M = E_R \times \left(\frac{w}{p}\right) \times (Pass-through\ rate) = E_R \times E_w^p$$

where E_M is the elasticity of the derived demand facing the manufacturer, E_R is the elasticity of final demand facing the retailer, and E^p_w is the elasticity of the retail price with respect to the wholesale price. This equation shows that in a retail environment, where one unit of the intermediate good (widgets) translates into one unit of output (widgets), the elasticity of the manufacturer's derived demand equals the elasticity of the retail demand times the ratio of the wholesale and retail prices, w/p, times the pass-through rate. The ratio of the wholesale and retail prices times the pass-through rate is just the elasticity of the retail price with respect to the wholesale price, as indicated by the last equality in the equation.

From this relationship we can derive several special cases of interest. If the retail market is perfectly competitive, then the retail price equals the retailer's marginal cost, and the pass-through rate equals 1 (because the retail price adjusts one-for-one with the wholesale price). Suppose we make the simplifying assumption that the wholesale price is the only source of marginal cost at the retail level. This assumption is almost never literally true, but it may be a reasonable approximation for products in which the wholesale price constitutes the majority of the retailer's marginal cost. Under this assumption, perfect competition between retailers yields $p=w$ (i.e., price equals marginal cost). In this special case, the equation above shows that the elasticity of the derived demand is equal to the elasticity of the retail demand. Of course, the retail markets in which scanner data are available are typically not *perfectly* competitive, and the wholesale price does not constitute 100 percent of the marginal cost incurred by retailers in selling most products.[26] Thus, the practical value of this special case seems remote.

If retailers set prices to maintain constant percentage mark-ups, then the elasticity of the retail price with respect to the wholesale price is equal to 1. Under this assumption, the equation above also shows that the derived demand elasticity equals the retail elasticity. Constant percentage mark-ups are profit maximizing for single-product retailers that face constant elasticity demand *and* incur no (marginal) costs other than the wholesale price.

---

[25] Formally, let $D_R(p)$ be the final demand facing a retailer for some product, where p is the retail price, and let w be the wholesale price the retailer pays the manufacturer for each unit that it purchases and resells to final consumers. Let $p(w)$ be the price the retailer charges given a wholesale price of w. The derived demand facing the manufacturer is then $D_M(w) = D_R(p(w))$. Differentiating D_M with respect to w, putting the expression in elasticity form, and recognizing that $D_M=D_R$ yields the expression in the text.

[26] Retail mark-ups over the wholesale price typically range from 20 to 80 percent, depending on the product, contradicting the implication that $p=w$ in this special case.

These are strong assumptions that might be plausible in some applications, but clearly not in all settings.

Outside of these special cases, the relationship between the elasticities at different levels in the production chain is not one-to-one. In general, the relationship depends on the shape of demand curves and the nature of competition. Given assumptions about these factors, it is possible to calculate the relationship. For example, in the special case of linear demand, a retail marginal cost of w, and monopoly at the manufacturer and retail levels, it can be shown that $w/p = 2/3$ and that the pass-through rate is ½. In this case the derived demand elasticity is one-third the retail elasticity. Other common demand curves (e.g., semi-log, AIDS, and constant elasticity) yield pass-through rates that exceed ½. The derived demand elasticity is closer to the retail elasticity in these cases than it is under linear demand, other factors equal.

The relationship becomes considerably more complicated for multi-product retailers that compete with one another. We discuss three complications here that relate to institutions that are prevalent in the retailing environment.

One complication is the "one-stop shopping" nature of retail outlets, which generates demand-side complementarities among products on the shelf that are unrelated to consumers underlying preferences for the products. For example, a lower price for milk might draw customers into the store where they then decide to purchase detergent while they are there. This makes milk and detergent complements in demand from the perspective of the grocery store, even though consumer preferences for these products are probably unrelated.

A second complication is the extensive use in retailing of frequent, but temporary discounts on alternative sets of products over time.[27] As far as we know, there has not been any work on how retail sales behavior affects the elasticities of the derived demand for the products they sell.[28] This issues was discussed above at the beginning of this section (Section V. A., 1-3).

A third complication that arises in the retailing environment is that retailers have scarce shelf space and can sometimes use this to their advantage to discipline the pricing behavior of suppliers. The reader may have noticed that in all of the examples we have discussed so far, the elasticity of demand facing the manufacturer of some product A is no larger than the elasticity facing retailers. This is the "normal" case for products that are not subject to the risk of being dropped from the shelf by retailers in response to a small increase in the wholesale price. However, if retailers can credibly threaten to remove a product from their shelves when faced with a price increase, the elasticity of demand for a product at the manufacturer level can exceed the elasticity at the retail level.

---

[27] *See*, for example, Hosken and Reiffen (2000).

[28] Sporadic sales behavior may also complicate the estimation of retail demand elasticities by inducing consumers to purchase products on sale and hold them in inventory. See the discussion on aggregation in section I.B.

A simple example illustrates this point. Imagine a market in which four manufacturers--- A, B, C, and D, compete for two "slots" at a retail outlet. To keep things simple, assume that the retailer is a monopolist, that the manufacturers have the same costs, and that all manufacturers know that their rivals have the same costs.[29] Assume further that the four products are symmetric in the sense the retailer expects to make the same sales and earn the same profits regardless of which two products it carries.[30] Manufacturers compete to have their products stocked by announcing their wholesale prices. The retailer then selects the two products it will carry, sets retail prices, and pays the winning manufacturers the wholesale prices that they announced for each unit sold.[31]

This situation is analogous to an auction in which four identical bidders, (the four manufacturers) "bid" for two identical items (the two slots on the shelf). Since there are more bidders than items, and the bidders have complete information about their rivals, this auction will yield the perfectly competitive outcome. That is, the bidding process will result in a wholesale price equal to the manufacturers' marginal cost. Suppose that the winning bidders are manufacturers A and B. What is the elasticity of the derived demand facing manufacturers A and B?

To answer this question, we need to consider what would happen if one of the winning bidders attempted to raise its wholesale price. Suppose that manufacturer A did so. Because the losing bidders, C and D, each stands ready to sell a product with a sales and profit potential equal to that of product A, the retailer would respond to A's price increase by replacing product A with product C or D. That is, a wholesale price increase by manufacturer A would cause it to lose *all* of its sales. This means that the elasticity of demand facing the manufacturer A is very high (in this example, infinite), even though the elasticity of the consumer demand for product A could be very low. The reason for the large own elasticity for product A is the high cross elasticity between product A and other products C and D that are not currently carried by the retailer.[32]

Now consider the effects of a merger between the two winning bidders, A and B. After the merger, there will still be three independent firms bidding for two slots. The post-merger auction will still yield the competitive outcome, so the merger will have *no* effect on the wholesale price. Notice that this conclusion is independent of the own and cross elasticities of the *consumer* demand (i.e., the demand facing retailers) for the merging firms' products.

---

[29] The insights from this example are relevant for more complicated markets.

[30] Note that this assumption does not mean that the products are homogenous. They could be differentiated or even independent products that have the same retail profit potential.

[31] In practice, competition for shelf space often involves more complicated payment schedules than simple linear prices (see the next section on nonlinear contracts). However, this simple example is rich enough to convey the point we want to make here.

This example shows that retail shelf-space constraints can have important implications for manufacturer-level demand elasticities. In particular, retail demand elasticities may understate manufacture-level elasticities if retailers respond to a wholesale price increase by dropping the manufacturer's product. Note that an important implicit assumption in this example is that the shelf space allocated to any one product is inelastic with respect to the product's profitability. For items that receive only one facing, this may be true, but for items that receive multiple facings, the space allocated to the product can be reduced if it becomes less profitable. The importance of shelf-space effects is likely to vary from case to case. The key question is whether the wholesale price charged by the manufacturer is constrained at the margin by the retailer's threat to drop the product from its shelves, or by the reduction in sales caused when the retailer passes part of the wholesale price increase on to consumers. We suspect that for some products where brand loyalty is not particularly strong, retailers' threats to displace products will provide strong disciplining effects on manufacturer price increases. In such cases, retail-level elasticities may understate manufacturer-level elasticities. On the other hand, some strong brands would not be dropped by retailers without a large increase in the wholesale price. In these cases, retail-level elasticities may overstate manufacturer-level elasticities.

Many of the demand system estimations presented to Agencies use the multi-stage budgeting approach with the AIDS (Almost Ideal Demand System) demand specification. The AIDS system is not of the constant elasticity form, and retailers nearly always sell multiple products. Thus, constant mark-ups generally do not reflect profit maximizing behavior by retailers in the AIDS analyses that are typically done, suggesting that the upstream and downstream elasticities will not be equal. A common response to this concern is an empirical observation that "retailers tend to follow constant mark-ups." However, economists are generally uncomfortable with models based on *ad hoc* assumptions like constant mark-ups without an explanation of how they emerge from rational behavior.[33] These studies also ignore the three complications just discussed---demand complementarities from one-stop shopping, retailer sales behavior, and retail shelf-space constraints. These issues clearly deserve more attention.

C. Nonlinear Payment Schedules

The foregoing discussion demonstrates that the relationship between the elasticities of derived and final demands is not straightforward. This complicates the chain of inference between retail demand estimation and the competitive effects of upstream mergers, even under linear pricing. This subsection considers a second factor that complicates the inference chain --- nonlinear payment schedules.

Nonlinearities are pervasive in the transactions that govern exchange in intermediate good markets. A simple example is a two-part tariff, which involves both a fixed fee and a per-unit wholesale price. Fixed fees can be positive (e.g., a franchise fee) or negative

---

[33] An explanation of the use of constant mark-ups when retail demand is of the AIDS form would appear to require some notion of bounded rationality.

(e.g., a slotting allowance)34. If the fixed fee is positive, the average payment declines with the amount purchased (quantity discount); if the fixed fee is negative, the average payment increases with the amount purchased (quantity premia). A wide range of fees exchanged by manufacturers and retailers affect the marginal and/or the fixed (or "inframarginal") payment from the retailer to the manufacturer. Examples include presentation fees (paid for the privilege of making a sales presentation); display fees (paid for special merchandising and the display of products);35 pay-to-stay fees (paid to have the retailer continue stocking and displaying a product); and failure fees (paid when a product does not meet expected goals). Other common components of nonlinear payment schedules include volume discounts, minimum and maximum purchase commitments, and liquidated damages.

The complication introduced by nonlinear payments goes beyond simply trying to draw inferences about derived demand elasticities from retail data. Competition in nonlinear payment schedules is fundamentally different from competition in per-unit prices. Perhaps the easiest way to see this is through a simple example, which is based on models examined by O'Brien and Shaffer (1997)[36] and Shaffer (1991). The example illustrates that nonlinear payment schedules can have important implications for the effects of mergers among upstream suppliers.

O'Brien and Shaffer consider a model in which two differentiated suppliers compete in nonlinear contracts to sell through a single retailer. The authors show that the equilibrium contracts involve nonlinear payments in which the *marginal* transfer price (the per-unit component) paid by the retailer for each unit purchased equals the manufacturer's marginal cost. For the special case of two-part tariff contracts, this means that the wholesale price equals the manufacturer's marginal cost. Thus, nonlinear pricing allows the upstream firms to avoid double-marginalization,[37] analogous to the well-known case of nonlinear pricing under bilateral monopoly.[38]

---

[34] Slotting allowances are payments from manufacturers to retailers to induce the retailer to shelve the product. The use of these fees is found throughout the food retailing industry. A related practice is that of "pay-to-stay" fees, which are made in periods subsequent to the initial stocking decision so that the retailer continues to shelve the manufacturer's products.

[35] Display fees are for special displays or favored placement. Examples include special end aisle displays, "display pyramids" (such as for 12-can boxes of soft drinks), and preferred position on shelves (e.g., eye-level for bread).

[36] See also Bernheim and Whinston (1998), who studied a similar model.

[37] "Double-marginalization" refers to the pricing distortion that occurs when a retailer adds its own (supra-competitive) mark-up to an upstream firm's own (supra-competitive) mark-up.

[38] A basic result in the economics of vertical control is that bilateral monopolists can avoid double-marginalization (cf. note 12) using two-part tariffs.

This result has important implications for the effects of upstream mergers when nonlinear contracts are feasible. Suppose the two upstream firms in the O'Brien/Shaffer model merge. The combined firm is a multi-product monopolist that can employ sophisticated contracts to sell through a downstream monopolist. This problem was analyzed formally by Shaffer (1991). He showed that the upstream firm (the merged firm in our context) cannot extract all the surplus from the retailer with standard nonlinear contracts in which the payments for each product depends only the amount purchased of that product. The reason for this is that the retail monopolist can credibly threaten to carry only one of the products if the manufacturer attempts to capture all of its surplus. Given this constraint, Shaffer finds that the merged firm will charge wholesale prices greater than marginal cost to capture some additional surplus, trading this benefit off against the cost of introducing double-marginalization. On the other hand, if the manufacturer can use more sophisticated contracts, such as aggregate rebates, full-line forcing, under which the retailer's payment for each product may depend on the amount purchased of both products, then the manufacturer will charge wholesale prices equal marginal cost. The idea is that by effectively bundling its products, through "aggregate rebates" (rebates based on the aggregate purchases) or full-line forcing (making the payment terms contingent on the purchase of both products), the monopolist is able to capture more surplus without introducing a double marginalization distortion.

Combining Shaffer's results with the result in O'Brien and Shaffer, we see that the effects of an upstream merger depend critically on the nature of the contracts employed by the manufacturers. If the merged firm is restricted to standard nonlinear contracts, the merger leads to an increase in wholesale prices. On the other hand, if the merged firm can employ more sophisticated contracts, such as aggregate rebates or full line forcing, then the merger will have no effect on wholesale prices. The only affect of the merger in the latter case is to transfer surplus from the retailer to the manufacturers. Since the wholesale price does not change, the retail price does not change either, so the merger has no effect on consumer welfare.[39]

---

[39] This is a rather extreme example because it ignores informational and contracting imperfections that might prevent firms from writing contracts that eliminate double-marginalization completely. However, the example does illustrate that nonlinear pricing may have important implications for the effects of upstream mergers.

The literature on competition in nonlinear contracts in intermediate good markets is still developing.[40] More work needs to be done, both theoretical and empirical, before we will be in a position to say with confidence how nonlinear pricing alters the effects of horizontal mergers. As the literature continues to advance in this area, the best strategy for merger analysis is probably to continue to employ models that assume linear pricing. We have no empirical basis at this point for concluding that the predictions of these models are inherently biased one way or another. Our intuition is that models based on linear pricing will probably overstate the anticompetitive effects of horizontal mergers, because multi-product nonlinear pricing tends to eliminate double marginalization distortions (as suggested by the example above). However, the precise nature and importance of any bias awaits additional theoretical and empirical work.

VI. CONCLUSION

Economists have made substantial progress in applying econometric techniques to the analysis of horizontal mergers. As a commentator recently observed, econometrics has much to offer as to means for "illuminating critical issues in antitrust investigations and litigation."[41] In this paper, we have attempted to identify some aspects of this approach that could benefit from additional analysis and research by both academic and practicing antitrust economists. We do not intend to indicate that we believe that econometric analyses of scanner data are not useful. At the FTC we regularly conduct such analyses and have found them to be useful, when combined with the other evidence developed in a merger investigation. This paper, however, has highlighted issues that in some contexts are likely to require specific attention in assessing the viability and utility of the estimates.

---

[40] The theoretical literature on buyer-specific nonlinear contracts has focused mainly on cases with oligopoly at either the upstream or downstream level and either a single seller or perfect competition at the other level. It has also focused on different issues than horizontal mergers. For example, O'Brien and Shaffer (1997) and Bernheim and Whinston (1998) examine incentives for exclusive dealing when the downstream firm is a monopolist. O'Brien and Shaffer (1992) and McAfee and Schwartz (1994) examine the role of vertical restraints and nondiscrimination clauses for a single supplier selling through competing retailers. Hart and Tirole (1990) consider buyer-specific contracting with duopoly at both stages, but they focus on the effects of vertical integration and exclusive contracts. There is no published empirical work on how to predict the effects of horizontal mergers when firms negotiate nonlinear contracts. An interesting step in this direction is taken by Villas-Boas (2001). She estimates the retail demand for yogurt using the discrete choice methodology of Berry (1994) and Barry, Levinsohn and Pakes (1995) and attempts to distinguish between different models of (linear and nonlinear) input pricing using a non-nested hypothesis test, as in Bresnahan (1987). Using this technique, it would be possible in principle to distinguish between different models of input pricing and to use that model to predict the effects of upstream mergers.

[41] Werden (2002), p. 47.

Bibliography

Abraham, Magid, and Leonard Lodish (1993). "An Implemented System for Improving Promotion Productivity using Store Scanner Data." *Marketing Science* 12 1993, 248-269.

Abrue, Dilip, Pearce, David, and Stacchetti, Enio (1986). "Optimal Cartel Equilibria with Imperfect Monitoring," *Journal of Economic Theory* 39, 251-69.

Bernheim, B. Douglas, and Michael Whinston (1998). "Exclusive Dealing," *Journal of Political Economy*, 106, 64-103.

Berry, Steven *et al.*(1995). "Automobile Prices in Market Equilibrium," *Econometrica*; 63, 841-90.

Berry, Steven (1994). "Estimating Discrete Choice Models of Product Differentiation," *Rand Journal of Economics* 25, 242-62.

Bertrand, Joseph (1883). Review of "Theorie Mathematique de la Richess Sociale" and Recherche sur les Principes Mathematiques de la Theorie des Richesses." *Journal de Savants*, 499-508.

Bresnahan, Timothy (1987). "Competition and Collusion in the American Automobile Industry: The 1955 Price War," *Journal of Industrial Economics* 35, 457-82.

Bresnahan, Timothy (1997). "Valuation of New Goods under Perfect and Imperfect Competition: Comment," in Bresnahan, Timothy and Gordon, Robert J., eds. *The Economics of New Goods: NBER Studies in Income and Wealth vol. 58.*, 237-47.

Bresnahan, Timothy (1997). "The Apple Cinnamon Cheerios War: Valuing New Goods, Identifying Market Power, and Economic Measurement," mimeo.

Brownstone, David and Robert Valletta (2001). "The Bootstrap and Multiple Imputations: Harnessing Increased Computing Power for Improved Statistical Tests," *Journal of Economic Perspectives* 15, 129-41.

Capps, Oral, *et al.* (2001), "Specification Issues and Confidence Intervals in Unilateral Price Effects Analysis," mimeo.

Cournot, Augustin (1987). *Researches sur les Principes Mathematiques de la Thoery des Richesses.* English edition (ed. N. Bacon): *Researches into the Mathematical Principles of the Theory of Wealth.* New York: Macmillan.

Crooke, Phillip *et al.* (1999). "Effects of Assumed Demand Form on Simulated Postmerger Equilibria," *Review of Industrial Organization* 15, 205-17.

Deaton, Angus, and John Muellbauer (1980). *Economics and Consumer Behavior*.

Efron, Bradley and Robert Tibshirani (1993). *An Introduction to the Bootstrap.* Monographs on Statistics and Applied Probability, v. 57.

Fershtman, Chaim and Pakes, Ariel (2000). "A Dynamic Oligopoly with Collusion and Price Wars," *Rand Journal of Economics*, 31, 207-236.

Fisher, Franklin (1989). "Games Economists Play," *RAND Journal of Economics* 20, 113-24.

Freedman, D. and Peters, S. (1984). "Bootstrapping a Regression Equation: Some Empirical Results," *Journal of the American Statistical Association* 79, 97-106.

Friedman, James (1971). "A Noncooperative Equilibrium for Supergames," *Review of Economic Studies* 38, 1-12.

Genesove, David and Wallace P. Mullin (1988). "Testing Static Oligopoly Models: Conduct and Cost in the Sugar Industry, 1890-1914," *Rand Journal of Economics*, 29 (1998), 355-77.

Goldberger, Arthur (1991). *A Course in Econometrics*.

Gorman, W. M. (1959). "Separable Utility and Aggregation," *Econometrica* 21, 469-481

Gowrisankaran, Gautam (1999). "A Dynamic Model of Endogenous Horizontal Mergers," *Rand Journal of Economics*, 30, 56-83.

Green, Edward, and Porter, Robert (1984). "Non-Cooperative Collusion Under Imperfect Price Information," *Econometrica* 52, 87-100.

Greene, William (1997). *Econometric Analysis (3rd ed.)*.

Hart, Oliver, and Jean Tirole (1990). "Vertical Integration and Market Foreclosure," *Brookings Papers on Economic Activity*, 205-276.

Hausman, Jerry *et al.* (1994). "Competitive Analysis with Differentiated Products," *Annales-d'Economie-et-de-Statistique*; 34, 159-80.

Hausman, Jerry (1997). "Valuation of New Goods under Perfect and Imperfect Competition," in Bresnahan, Timothy and Gordon, Robert J., eds. *The Economics of New Goods: NBER Studies in Income and Wealth vol. 58.*, 209-37.

Hausman, Jerry and Gregory Leonard (1997), "Economic Analysis of Differentiated Products Mergers Using Real World Data," *George Mason Law Review* 5 (1997), 321-43.

Hausman, Jerry and Gregory Leonard (2000). "The Competitive Effects of a New Product Introduction: A Case Study," Mimeo, MIT.

Hendel, Igal and Aviv Nevo (2001). "Sales and Consumer Inventory." unpublished manuscript.

Hoch, Stephen, Byung-Do Kim, Alan Montgomery, and Peter Rossi (1995). "Determinants of Store-Level Price Elasticity." *Journal of Marketing Research* 23, 17-29.

Horn, Heinrick, and Asher Wolinsky (1988). "Bilateral Monopolies and Incentives for Merger," *Rand Journal of Economics*, 19, 408-419.

Hosken, Daniel, and David Reiffen (1999). "Pricing Behavior of Multiproduct Retailers" *Federal Trade Commission Bureau of Economics Working Paper* 225

Irwin, Douglas, and Nina Pavcnik (2001). "Airbus Versus Boeing Revisited: International Competition in the Aircraft Market," mimeo. (http://www.dartmouth.edu/~npavcnik/Research_files/airbus.pdf).

Katz, Michael and Carl Shapiro (1986). "Consumer Shopping Behavior in the Retail Coffee Market," in P. Ippolito and D. Scheffman (eds.) *Empirical Approaches to Consumer Protection Economics*, FTC, March 1986, 415-443.

Koenker, Roger, and Kevin Hallock (2001). "Quantile Regression," *Journal of Economic Perspectives* 15, 143-56.

Maskin, Eric and Jean Tirole (1987). "A Theory of Dynamic Oligopoly, III: Cournot Competition," *European Economic Review* 31, 947-68.

Maskin, Eric and Jean Tirole (1988a), "A Theory of Dynamic Oligopoly I: Overview and Quantity Competition With Large Fixed Costs," *Econometrica*, 56, 549-69.

Maskin, Eric and Jean Tirole (1988b), "A Theory of Dynamic Oligopoly II: Price Competition, Kinked Demand Curves, and Edgeworth Cycles," *Econometrica*, 56, 571-99.

Montgomery, Alan (1997). "Creating Micro-Marketing Pricing Strategies Using Supermarket Scanner Data." *Marketing Science* 16, 315-337.

Nash, John F. (1950). "Non-cooperative Games," *Econometrica*, 18, 155-62.

Nevo, Aviv (2000). "Mergers with Differentiated Products: The Case of the Ready-to-Eat Cereal Industry," *Rand Journal of Economics*, 31, 395-421.

Nevo, Aviv (2001). "Measuring Market Power in the Ready-to-Eat Cereal Industry," *Econometrica*, 69, 307-342.

McAfee, R. Preston, and Marius Schwartz (1994). "Opportunism in Multilateral Vertical Contracting, Nondiscrimination, Exclusivity, and Uniformity," *American Economic Review,* 84, 210-30.

Novshek, William (1980). "Cournot Equilibrium with Free Entry," *Review of Economic Studies*, 47, 473-86.

O'Brien, Daniel P. and Greg Shaffer (1992). "Vertical Control with Bilateral Contracts," *Rand Journal of Economics*, 23, 299-308.

O'Brien, Daniel P. and Greg Shaffer (1997). "Nonlinear Supply Contracts, Exclusive Dealing, and Equilibrium Market Foreclosure," *Journal of Economics & Management Strategy*, 6, 755-785.

Pakes, Ariel and McGuire, P. (1994). "Computing Markov-Perfect Nash Equilibrium: Numerical Implications of a Dynamic Differentiated Product Model," *Rand Journal of Economics*, 25, 555-589.

Pesendorfer, Martin (2002). "Retail Sales: A Study of Pricing Behavior in Super Markets," *Journal of Business* 75, 33-66.

Pinkse, Joris and Slade, Margaret (2001). "Mergers, Brand Competition, and the Price of a Pint," Mimeo, Department of Economics, University of British Columbia.

Pinkse, Joris, Slade, Margaret and Craig Brett (2002). "Spatial Price Competition," *Econometrica,* forthcoming.

Reiss, Peter and Matthew White (2001). "Household Electricity Demand, Revisited," *National Bureau of Economics Working Paper #8687*

Rotemberg, Julio, and Saloner, Garth (1986). "A Supergame-theoretic Model of Price Wars During Booms," *American Economic Review* 76, 390-407.

Sansolo, Michael (1992). "The Real Power of Promotion." *Progressive Grocer* 71, 36-41.

Scheffman, David (1992). "Statistical Measures of Market Power: Uses and Abuses," *Antitrust Law Journal* 60, 901-19.

Scheffman, David, and Spiller, Pablo (1996). "Econometric Market Delineation," *Managerial and Decision Economics* 17, 165-78.

Shaffer, Greg (1991). "Capturing Strategic Rent: Full-Line Forcing, Brand Discounts, Aggregate Rebates, and Maximum Resale Price Maintenance," *Journal of Industrial Economics* 39, 557-75.

Shapiro, Carl (1989). "The Theory of Business Strategy," *RAND Journal of Economics* 20, 125-37.

Slade, Margaret (2001). "Assessing Market Power in UK Brewing," Department of Economics, The University of British Columbia, Discussion Paper No. 01-04, March 2001.

Steiner, Robert L. (1973). "Does Advertising Lower Consumer Prices?" *Journal of Marketing*, 37(4).

Steiner, Robert L. (1993). "The Inverse Association Between the Margins of Manufacturers and Retailers," *Review of Industrial Organization*, 8(6), 717-40.

Steiner, Robert L. (2001). "A Dual-Stage View of the Consumer Goods Economy," *Journal of Economic Issues*, 35(1), 27-44.

Stigler, George (1964). "A Theory of Oligopoly," *Journal of Political Economy*, 72, 44-61.

Thomas, Charles (2001). "Collusion and Optimal Reserve Prices in Repeated Procurement Auctions," *Federal Trade Commission Bureau of Economics Working Paper No. 242*

Varian, Hal R. (1980), "A Model of Sales", *American Economic Review*; 70, 651-659.

Villas-Boas, Sofia Berto (2001). "Vertical Contracts Between Manufacturers and Retailers: An Empirical Analysis," Mimeo, University of California, Berkeley.

Werden, Gregory, and Luke Froeb (1994). "The Effects of Mergers in Differentiated Products Industries: Logit Demand and Merger Policy," *Journal of Law, Economics, & Organization* 10, 407-26.

Werden, Gregory et al. (1996). "The Use of the Logit Model in Applied Industrial Organization," *International Journal of the Economics of Business* 3, 83-105.

Werden, Gregory (2002). "A Perspective on the Use of Econometrics in Merger Investigations and Litigation," *Antitrust* forthcoming

Werden, Gregory (1997). "Simulating the Effects of Differentiated Products Mergers: A Practitioner's Guide," in Julie Caswell and Ronald Cotterill, eds., *Strategy and Policy in the Food System: Emerging Issues*.

Wolfram, Catherine (1999). "Measuring Duopoly Power in the British Electricity Spot Market," *American Economic Review*, 89, 805-26.